MAGNIFY THE LORD

SCRIPTURE SONGS FOR CHOIR OR CONGREGATION

ARRANGED FOR USE IN MEDLEYS OR INDIVIDUALLY
BY TOM FETTKE

Compiled by Ken Bible and Tom Fettke

D1004297

Lillenas Publishing Co.
KANSAS CITY, MO. 64141

*Magnify the Lord Medley

O MAGNIFY THE LORD: v.1, unison; v.2, parts (to the end of the song).   *Arr. by Tom Fettke*
BECAUSE OF WHO YOU ARE: 1st time, solo; 2nd time, unison choir.
LET THERE BE PRAISE: 1st chorus, div.; v.1, unison ladies; 2nd chorus, div.; v.2, choir unison; last
   chorus, div., use medley ending.

O Magnify the Lord

M. T. and D. T.   (Ps. 34:3; Rev. 19:16)   MELODIE and DICK TUNNEY

Lord, O mag - ni - fy____ the Lord, and may His name be
King; O wor-ship Christ,_ the King; and may His name be

lift - ed__high for - ev - er! 2. O er!

King of__ Kings and Lord__ of__ Lords, ____ may His name be

lift - ed__high for - ev - er! 1. O ev - er!

ev - er!_____

Because of Who You Are

(Ps. 99:5)

B. F. and B. S.

BOB FARRELL and BILLY SMILEY

Let There Be Praise

(Ps. 22:3; 136:1; 148:13; 149:1-2, 5)

M. T. and D. T.

MELODIE and DICK TUNNEY

Let there be praise, let there be joy in our hearts.

Sing to the Lord, give Him the glo - ry (glo - ry);

Let there be praise, let there be joy in our hearts.

For - ev - er - more let His love fill the air, and let there be

praise.

1. He in - hab-its the praise of His peo-ple, and dwells deep with -
2. When the Spir-it of God is with - in us, we will o - ver -

in. The___ peace that He gives none can e - qual; His___ love, it knows no
come. In our weak-ness His strength will de - fend us when His praise is on our

end.
tongue. So lift your voic - es; with glad-ness sing.

Pro-claim through all the earth___ that Je - sus Christ is King! King!

CODA - Medley ending

praise! Let there,___ O let there___ be praise!

Keyboard

*Our God Reigns Medley

Arr. by Tom Fettke

WE WILL GLORIFY: v.1, choir div.; v.2, men unison; v.3, ladies unison; v.4, choir div. (add descant)
I LOVE YOU, LORD: Choir div.
OUR GOD REIGNS: v.1, choir unison; all refrains div.; v.2, solo; v.5, choir unison; use choral medley tag.

We Will Glorify

(Ex. 3:13; Rev. 4:8-11, 5:8-14, 17:14)

TWILA PARIS
Descant by Tom Fettke

T. P.

♩ = 84   *Descant - last stanza*

Hal - le - lu - jah!   Hal - le - lu -

1. We will glo-ri-fy the King of Kings; we will glo-ri-fy the___
2. Lord Je - ho-vah reigns in maj-es-ty; we will bow be-fore His___
3. He is Lord of heav-en, Lord of earth; He is Lord of all who___
4. Hal-le - lu-jah to the King of Kings; hal-le - lu-jah to the___

Song ending

jah!   Hal-le-lu-jah to the Lord of lords, who___ is the great I Am.

Suggested introduction

Lamb; We will glo-ri-fy the Lord of Lords, who___ is the great I Am.
throne, We will wor-ship Him in right-teous-ness; we will worship Him a-lone.
live. He is Lord a-bove the u - ni-verse; all___ praise to Him we give.
Lamb; Hal-le - lu-jah to the Lord of Lords, who___ is the great I Am.

8

Medley ending

I Love You, Lord
(Ps. 116:1-2, 145:1-2)

L. K.

LAURIE KLEIN
Arr. by Eugene Thomas

I love You, Lord,____ and I lift my voice____ To wor - ship You; O my soul, re - joice! Take joy, my King,____ in____ what You hear;____ May it be a sweet, sweet____ sound in__Your ear.____

Our God Reigns

L. E. S. Jr.

(Is. 52:7; 53; Luke 24:5-6, 39)

LEONARD E. SMITH, Jr.
Arr. by Tom Fettke

1. How love-ly on the moun-tains are the feet of him
2. He had no state - ly form, He had no maj - es-ty
3. It was our sin and guilt that bruised and wound-ed Him.
4. Meek as a lamb that's led out to the slaugh-ter-house,
5. Out from the tomb He came with grace and maj - es-ty;

Who brings good news, good news;
That we should be drawn to Him.
It was our sin that brought Him down.
Dumb as a sheep be - fore its shearer,
He is a - live, He is a - live.

An - nounc-ing peace, pro - claim - ing news of
He was de - spised and we took no ac-
When we like sheep had gone a - stray our
His life ran down up - on the ground like
God loves us so, see here His hands, His

*King of Kings Medley

Arr. by Tom Fettke

SING HALLELUJAH (to the Lord): 1st time, unison choir (no descant); 2nd time, ladies sing melody, men sing descant.

KING OF KINGS: 1st time, unison choir; 2nd time sing 2 part round—use an equal number of men and women on each part.

WE BOW DOWN: v. 1 and Refrain, div.; v.2, ladies 2 part; Refrain, all div.

Sing Hallelujah (to the Lord)

L. S.   (Rev. 19:6)   LINDA STASSEN

lu - jah, Sing hal-le-lu-jah to the Lord.

sing hal-le-lu - jah, Sing hal-le-lu-jah to the Lord.

Song and Medley ending

King of Kings

(Is. 9:6; Rev. 19:16)

SOPHIE CONTY and NAOMI BATYA

Ancient Hebrew Folksong

♩ = 104

2-part Round (optional)

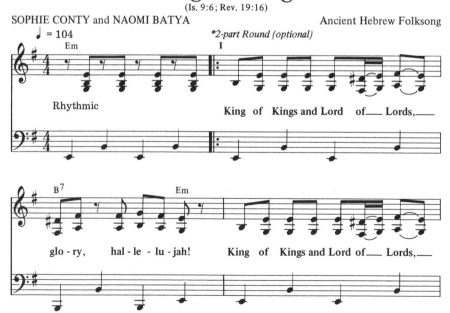

Rhythmic

King of Kings and Lord of Lords,

glo - ry, hal - le - lu - jah! King of Kings and Lord of Lords,

*Measures 2-5 are repeated on the orchestral tape trax (on the repeat) in order to complete the round.

glo - ry, hal - le - lu - jah! Je - sus, Prince of Peace, ___

glo - ry, hal - le - lu - jah! Je - sus, Prince of Peace, ___

Song and Medley ending

2nd time fine

Medley transition to "We Bow Down"

glo - ry, hal - le - lu - jah!

New tempo ♩ = 168

We Bow Down

(Ps. 95:6-7; Eph. 3:14-15; Phil. 2:9-11; Rev. 17:14)

T.P.

TWILA PARIS

1. You are___ Lord of cre-a - tion and Lord of my___
(2. You are___) King of cre-a - tion and King of my___

life, Lord of the land___ and the___ sea.___
life, King of the land___ and the___ sea.___

You were___ Lord of the heav - en be - fore there was___
You were___ King of the heav - en be - fore there was___

time, and Lord of all___ lords You will be!
time, and King of all___ kings You will be!

*Comfort Medley

Arr. by Tom Fettke

HE GIVETH MORE GRACE: Use suggested introduction; v.1 and Refrain, choir div.; v.2, solo; Refrain, choir div.
GOT ANY RIVERS?: Div., a cappella preferred. See note after song regarding tape trax.
HE WILL CARRY YOU: Choir div. until D.S.; at D.S., choir unison; Refrain, div. to end.

He Giveth More Grace

(Is. 40:31; Rom. 5:17, 20-21; 2 Cor. 9:8; 12:9; Eph. 3:5; Phil. 4:19)

ANNIE JOHNSON FLINT   HUBERT MITCHELL

1. He giv-eth more grace when the bur-dens grow great-er; He
2. When we have ex-haust-ed our store of en-dur-ance, When

send-eth more strength when the la-bors in-crease. To
our strength has failed ere the day is half done, When

add-ed af-flic-tion He add-eth His mer-cy; To mul-ti-plied
we reach the end of our hoard-ed re-sourc-es, Our Fa-ther's full

tri-als, His mul-ti-plied peace. REFRAIN His love has no lim-it; His
giv-ing is on-ly be-gun.

grace has no mea-sure; His power has no bound-a-ry known un-to men.

Suggested introduction

For out of His in-fi-nite rich-es in Je-sus, He

Song ending / **Medley ending**

giv-eth, and giv-eth, and giv-eth a-gain! giv-eth a-gain!

Got Any Rivers?

(Matt. 17:20)

O. E.

OSCAR ELIASON

*See note at end of chorus regarding orchestral trax.

Got an-y riv-ers you think are un-cross-a-ble? Got an-y

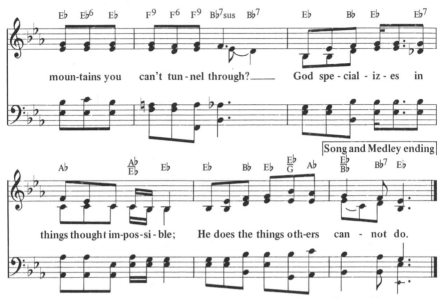

moun-tains you can't tun-nel through?____ God spe - cial - iz - es in

Song and Medley ending

things thought im-pos-si-ble; He does the things oth-ers can - not do.

This selection is not included on the orchestral trax tape, a cappella is preferred. Tape machine operator must stop tape after "He Giveth More Grace". Upon completion of "Got Any Rivers" start the tape for "He Will Carry You". If needed use live keyboard as accompaniment for "Got Any Rivers".

He Will Carry You

(Is. 40:11; 46:3-4; Matt. 11:28; 17:20)

S. W. B.

SCOTT WESLEY BROWN

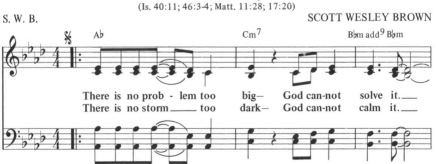

There is no prob - lem too big— God can-not solve it.____
There is no storm____ too dark— God can-not calm it.____

car-ried the weight of the world___ up-on His shou - der,

shoul - der,___ I know, my sis - ter, that He will car - ry

you.___ He said, "Come un - to Me

all who are wea - ry and I will

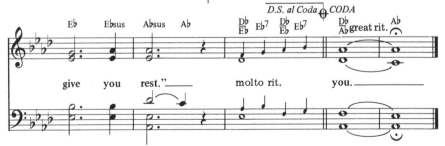

give you rest."___ molto rit. you.___

*His Name Medley

Arr. by Tom Fettke

EMMANUEL: Choir unison
JESUS, NAME ABOVE ALL NAMES: First time, ladies unison; second time, all unison
HIS NAME IS WONDERFUL: Choir, div.; D.S. a cappella preferred, slowly

Emmanuel
(Matt. 1:23)

B. McG.

BOB McGEE

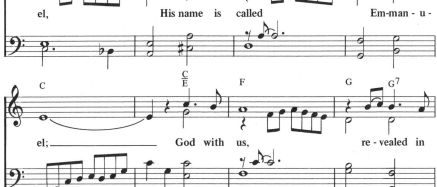

us; His name is called Em - man - u -

Song ending | Medley ending

el. el.

Jesus, Name Above All Names

(Matt. 1:21-23; Phil. 2:9-11)

N. H.

NAIDA HEARN

Je - sus, name a - bove all names; beau-ti-ful

Sav - ior, glo - ri - ous Lord. Em -

man - u - el, God _ is with us; bless-ed Re-deem - er,

1,2 Song ending *2nd time Fine* | **2 Medley ending**

Liv - ing Word._____ Word._____

His Name Is Wonderful

(Is. 9:6; Acts 13:20)

A. M.   AUDREY MIEIR

His name is Won-der-ful,_____ His name is Won-der-ful,

His name is Won-der-ful, Je - sus, my Lord._____ He is the

might-y King,_____ Mas - ter of ev-'ry-thing; His name is Won-der-ful,

*Heaven Medley

Arr. by Tom Fettke

WE SHALL WALK THROUGH THE VALLEY: v.1, choir div.; v.4, ladies unison 1st line, men unison 2nd line, all div. 3rd and 4th lines.
SOON AND VERY SOON: v.1, choir div.; v.2, trio (sop., alt., ten.) or choir unison; v.3, all div.; v.4, choir unison—div. on "hallelujahs".
LOOKIN' FOR THE CITY: Refrain, div.; verse, solo (or choir unison); Refrain, div.

We Shall Walk Through the Valley

(Ps. 23:4; Rev. 21:3-4)

Traditional   Traditional

Song ending

We shall walk thro' the val - ley in peace.
There will be no sor - row there.
We shall meet our loved ones there.
We shall meet our Sav - ior there.

Medley ending

there. accel.

$\bullet = 63$

Soon and Very Soon

(Rev. 21:1-4)

ANDRAÉ CROUCH

A. C.

$\bullet = 63$

1. Soon and ver - y soon we are goin' to see the King.
2. No more cry - in' there, we are goin' to see the King.
3. No more dy - in' there, we are goin' to see the King.
4. Soon and ver - y soon we are goin' to see the King.

Soon and ver - y soon we are goin' to see the King.
No more cry - in' there, we are goin' to see the King.
No more dy - in' there, we are goin' to see the King.
Soon and ver - y soon we are goin' to see the King.

Lookin' for the City

(2 Cor. 5:1-8; Heb. 11:8-10, 13-16)

M. T., D. T. and B. D.

MELODIE and DICK TUNNEY
and BEVERLY DARNALL

I'm look-in' for the cit - y with the true foun-da - tion: A home in the heav-ens not made by hands.__ Its de - sign-er and build - er is the Lord of the a - ges; He pre - pared it for me__ be - fore the world __ be - gan. __ Since the mo - ment of new birth I've been a

*Call upon the Lord Medley

Arr. by Tom Fettke

UNTO THEE, O LORD: Use suggested introduction; v.1, all unison throughout (mixed voices sing descant);
  v.3, ladies unison (men sing descant)
DAY BY DAY: Div.
I WILL CALL UPON THE LORD: Men unison (ladies sing descant)

Unto Thee, O Lord

Based on Psalm 25:1-6   CHARLES F. MONROE

32

Day by Day

St. Richard of Chichester

(Ps. 25:4-5; 27:4)

TOM FETTKE

Day by day, dear Lord, three things I pray: To see Thee more clear-ly, love Thee more dear-ly, Fol-low Thee more near - ly, day by day.

Medley ending
New tempo ♩ = 122

I Will Call upon the Lord

(2 Sam. 22:47; Ps. 18:3)

Adapted by M. O'S.

MICHAEL O'SHIELDS

I will call up-on the Lord

I will call up-on the Lord who is wor-thy to be

who is wor-thy to be praised. So shall I be

praised. So shall I be saved from my en-e-mies.

saved from my en-e-mies.__ I will call up-on the Lord. Lord. The

_____ I will call up-on the Lord. Lord. The

Lord liv-eth, and bless-ed be the Rock; And let the God of my sal-va-tion be ex-

alt - ed. The Lord liv-eth, and bless-ed be the Rock; And let the God of

my sal-va-tion be ex - alt - ed. The ed.

*Bow Down
and Worship Medley

Arr. by Tom Fettke

COME, LET US WORSHIP AND BOW DOWN: 1st time, solo; 2nd time, unison choir.
WE WORSHIP AND ADORE YOU: Choir div.
ALLELUIA TO THE KING: Choir div.

Come, Let Us Worship
and Bow Down

Adapted by D. D.   (Ps. 95:6-7)   DAVE DOHERTY

Mak - er. Mak - er. For He ____ is our

God, and we are the peo-ple of His pas - ture and the

sheep ____ of His hand, just the sheep ____ of His

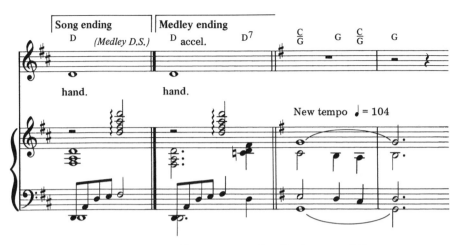

We Worship and Adore You

(Ps. 95:1-2, 6-7)

Traditional

Traditional

We wor-ship and a-dore You, Bow-ing down be-fore You, Songs of prais-es sing-ing, Hal-le-lu-jahs ring-ing. Hal-le-lu-jah, hal-le-lu-jah,—

hal - le - lu - jah, A - men. men.

Alleluia to the King

(Ps. 95:6; 99:9; Rev. 4:11)

MOSIE LISTER

M. L.

Be - cause God is ho - ly, I will bow down be -

fore__ Him. Be - cause He is ho - ly, His name I a -

dore. Be - cause God is wor - thy, He a - lone is

*Born Again Medley

Arr. by Tom Fettke

BORN AGAIN: v.1 and Refrain, div.; v.2, ladies duet (or 2 part ladies choir); Refrain, div.
I'M SO GLAD: v.1, choir unison; v.2, choir div.
A NEW NAME IN GLORY: v.1 and Refrain, choir div.; v.3, solo or choir unison; Refrain, choir div.

Born Again

(John 3:1-3)

ANDREW CULVERWELL

1. You may think it fool-ish what I'm gon-na say;
2. One man came to Je-sus (John and chap-ter three)

I'm not a-shamed, no, not a-shamed.
and so a-fraid, oh, so a-fraid:

One day I prayed, "Je-sus, take my sin a-way," And
"Mas-ter, You're from God, I real-ly do be-lieve." And

41

I'm So Glad

(Ps. 40:1-3; Luke 13:16)

Traditional

Traditional
Arr. by Tom Fettke

A New Name in Glory

C. A. M.

(Luke 10:20; 15:7; Rev. 3:5)

C. AUSTIN MILES

1. I was once a sin-ner, but I came Par-don to re-ceive
2. I was hum-bly kneel-ing at the cross, Fear-ing naught but God's
3. In the Book 'tis writ-ten, "Saved by Grace." O the joy that came

from my Lord.____ This was free-ly giv-en, and I found
an-gry frown,____ When the heav-ens o-pened and I saw
to my soul!____ Now I am for-giv-en, and I know

That He al-ways kept His word.
That my name was writ-ten down. There's a new name
By the blood I am made whole.

writ-ten down in glo-ry,____ And it's mine, O yes, it's
And it's mine,

44

mine!   And the   white-robed an-gels sing the   sto-ry,___ "A
yes, it's mine,

sin - ner has come   home."   For there's a   new name
has come home."

writ-ten down in   glo-ry,___ And it's   mine,   O yes, it's
And it's mine,

mine!   With my   sins for-giv-en I am   bound for heav-en,
yes, it's mine!

Song ending

Nev - er-more to   roam.

Choral medley ending

Nev - er-more to   roam.

*The Cross Medley

Arr. by Tom Fettke

WHEN I SURVEY: v.1, choir div.; v.2, ladies unison until "All the vain", men unison from there to the end.; v.4, choir unison
I LOVE HIM: Choir div. throughout
I WILL GLORY IN THE CROSS: v.1, solo; Refrain, choir div.; v.2 and Refrain, choir div.

When I Survey

ISAAC WATTS   (John 19:2, 34; Gal. 6:14; Phil. 3:7-10)   LOWELL MASON

1. When I sur - vey the___ won - drous__ Cross On which the Prince of___ Glo - ry died,___ My rich - est gain I___ count but __ loss, And pour con - tempt on all my___ pride.
2. For - bid it, Lord, that__ I___ should_ boast, Save in the death of___ Christ, my__ God.__ All the vain things that__ charm me__ most, I sac - ri - fice_ them to His__ blood.
3. See, from His head, His__ hands,_ His_ feet, Sor - row and love flow__ min - gled__ down.__ Did e'er such love and__ sor - row__ meet, Or thorns com - pose_ so rich a__ crown?
4. Were the whole realm of___ na - ture__ mine, That were a pres - ent__ far_ too_ small.__ Love so a - maz - ing,___ so__ di - vine, De - mands my soul, my life, my__ all. all.

Song ending | Medley ending

I Love Him

Traditional

(1 John 4:10, 19)

TOM FETTKE

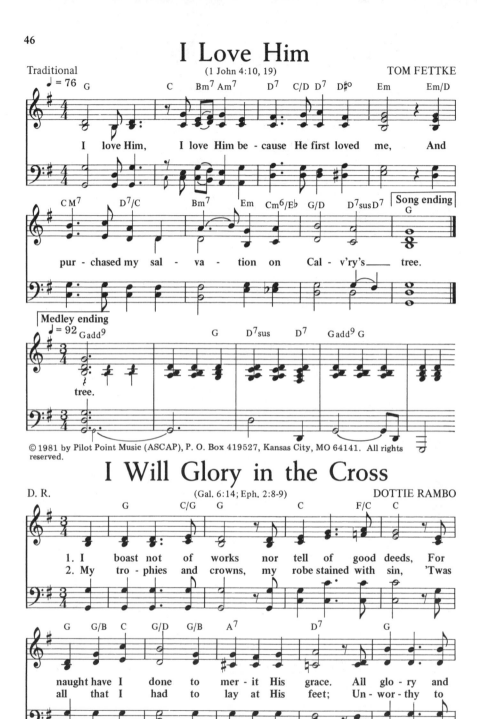

I love Him, I love Him be - cause He first loved me, And pur - chased my sal - va - tion on Cal - v'ry's___ tree.

Song ending

Medley ending

tree.

I Will Glory in the Cross

D. R.

(Gal. 6:14; Eph. 2:8-9)

DOTTIE RAMBO

1. I boast not of works nor tell of good deeds, For
2. My tro - phies and crowns, my robe stained with sin, 'Twas

naught have I done to mer - it His grace. All glo - ry and
all that I had to lay at His feet; Un - wor - thy to

47

*Come and Praise Medley

Arr. by Tom Fettke

DOXOLOGY: Use suggested introduction; choir div. throughout
O COME, LET US ADORE HIM: v.1, ladies unison; v.3, men unison; v.4, choir div.
COME, CHRISTIANS, JOIN TO SING: v.1, choir div.; v.2, choir unison; choral tag div.

Doxology

(Ps. 103:20-22)

THOMAS KEN

Old 100th
Attributed to Louis Bourgeois
Genevan Psalter

O Come, Let Us Adore Him

(Rom. 11:36; Rev. 5:11-14)

Traditional

Wade's *Cantus Diversi*

1. O come, let us a- dore Him. O come, let us a- dore Him. O come, let us a- dore Him, Christ the Lord.
2. We'll praise His name for- ev- er. We'll praise His name for- ev- er. We'll praise His name for- ev- er, Christ the Lord.
3. We'll give Him all the glo- ry. We'll give Him all the glo- ry. We'll give Him all the glo- ry, Christ the Lord.
4. For He a- lone is wor- thy; For He a- lone is wor- thy; For He a- lone is wor- thy, Christ the Lord.

Song ending | Medley ending

slight accel.

Come, Christians, Join to Sing

(Ps. 30:4; 67:3; 95:1-2; Heb. 13:15; Rev. 5:11-14)

CHRISTIAN HENRY BATEMAN

Source Unknown

1. Come, Chris- tians, join to sing— Al- le- lu- ia!
2. Come, lift your hearts on high— Al- le- lu- ia!
3. Praise yet our Christ a- gain— Al- le- lu- ia!

50

*Lamb Medley

Arr. by Tom Fettke

WORTHY IS THE LAMB: Choir div.
BEHOLD THE LAMB: Unison until "For sinners", sing parts there to end.
LAMB OF GLORY: v. 1; solo (or ladies unison); Refrain, choir div.; v.2; choir unison; Refrain, choir div.,
  use medley ending.

Worthy Is the Lamb

Adapted by D. W.

(Rev. 5:12)

DON WYRTZEN

glo - ry and bless - ing!_____ Wor - thy is the Lamb,

Wor - thy is the Lamb, Wor - thy is the Lamb that was

Song and Medley ending

slain,_____ Wor - thy is the Lamb!_____

Medley: segue to "Behold the Lamb"

Behold the Lamb

(John 1:29; Rev. 5:6, 9; 13:8)

D. R.

DOTTIE RAMBO
Arr. by Lee Herrington

Be - hold the Lamb,_____ be - hold the Lamb,_____

Slain from the foun - da - tion of the world._____ For sin - ners_____

cru - ci -fied,____ O ho - ly____ sac - ri -fice;____ Be-hold the Lamb of God,

Song and Medley ending   Rubato

____ be - hold   the   Lamb.____   Medley interlude

Lamb of Glory

(John 1:29; Heb. 9:22; Rev. 5:8-14)

G. N. and P. M.

GREG NELSON and PHILL McHUGH
Arr. by Tom Fettke

1. Hear the sto - ry____ from God's Word That kings   and priests   and
2. On   the cross God____ loved the world, While all   the pow'rs   of

proph - ets_ heard: There   would be   a   sac - ri - fice, And
hell   were hurled.   No   one there could un - der-stand The

54

*It Is Finished Medley

Arr. by Tom Fettke

IT IS FINISHED: Refrain, div.; Verse, unison; repeat Refrain, div.; 2nd time to Coda.
I LIVE: Div. throughout
CHRIST, THE LORD, IS RISEN TODAY: v.1, div.; v.3, ladies unison, first phrase, men unison,
   2nd phrase; parts from there on; sing opt. choral tag.

It Is Finished
(Is. 40:31; John 14:1; 19:30)

P. N. and S. W. B.   PHIL NAISH and SCOTT WESLEY BROWN

It   is   fin - ished;   Christ   has   won!____   It   was

writ - ten   of   God's   Son!   For be - hold____   the   Lamb   has ful-

Medley - 2nd time to Coda

filled   God's   plan;   And   it   is   fin - ished, and   He_has just be-

56

Song ending · *Fine*

VERSE · *Unison*

gun! Let not your heart be trou-bled; the vic-to-ry is yours. Je-sus Christ has won it; your tears shall be no more. So run and not be wea-ry, walk and nev-er fall; Lift up your voice to heav-en: crown Him Lord of all!

Medley - *D.S. al Coda*

D.S. al Fine

CODA

gun!

accel.

I Live

(John 14:19; Rom. 6:4-6)

R. C.

RICH COOK

I live, I live be-cause He is ris-en. I live, I live with
live, I live be-cause He is ris-en. I live, I live to

pow'r o-ver sin. I
wor - ship

Him. Thank You, Je - sus; thank You, Je - sus. Be-

cause You're a - live, be-cause You're a - live, be-cause You're a - live, ___ I

Song ending | Medley ending | New tempo ♩ = 112

live! | live. ___

Christ, the Lord, Is Risen Today

CHARLES WESLEY   (Matt. 28:6; 1 Cor. 15:20-22, 55)   from *Lyra Davidica*, 1708

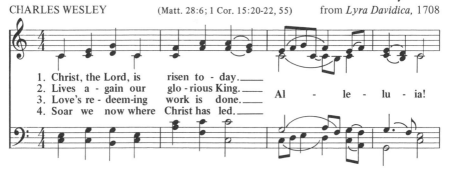

1. Christ, the Lord, is   risen to - day. ___
2. Lives a - gain our   glo - rious King. ___   Al - le - lu - ia!
3. Love's re - deem-ing   work is   done. ___
4. Soar we   now where   Christ has led. ___

Sons of men and an - gels say: ___
Where, O death, is now_ thy sting? ___
Fought the fight, the bat - tle won. ___
Fol - lowing our ex - alt - ed Head, ___

Al - le - lu - ia!

Raise your joys and tri - umphs high.
Dy - ing once, He all doth save.
Death in vain for - bids Him rise.
Made like Him, like Him we rise.

Al - le - lu - ia!

Song and
Medley ending

Sing, _ ye _ heavens, and, earth, re - ply, ___
Where thy _ vic - to - ry, O grave? ___
Christ has _ o - pened par - a - dise. ___
Ours _ the _ cross, the grave, the skies. ___

Al - le - lu - ia!

Optional choral tag

Al - le - lu - ia!   Al - le - lu - ia!

*Exalt Him Medley

Arr. by Tom Fettke

I EXALT THEE: Unison; div. at "I exalt Thee"
GLORIFY THY NAME: v.1, div.
BE EXALTED, O GOD: Unison until "For Thy steadfast", divide from there to end. Use opt. choral tag.

I Exalt Thee

(Ps. 97:9)

Adapted by P. S.

PETE SANCHEZ, Jr.

Glorify Thy Name

(Matt. 12:28; Rom. 15:6)

D. A.

DONNA ADKINS

1. Fa - ther, we love You, we wor - ship and a - dore You;
2. Je - sus, we love You, we wor - ship and a - dore You;
3. Spir - it, we love You, we wor - ship and a - dore You;

Glo - ri - fy Thy name in all the earth._____ Glo - ri - fy Thy

name, glo - ri - fy Thy name,_____ Glo - ri - fy Thy

Song ending

name in all the earth._____

Medley ending

♩ = 104

earth._____

Be Exalted, O God

Adapted by B. C.   (Ps. 57:9-11)   BRENT CHAMBERS

*Bless the Lord Medley

Arr. by Tom Fettke

BLESS HIS HOLY NAME: Divisi; 1st "He has", men unison; 2nd "He has", ladies unison; 3rd "He has", all div. to end.

BLESS THE LORD, O MY SOUL: 1st time, all unison; 2nd time, all div.

I WILL BLESS THE LORD: Unison or 3 parts until "the Lord is gracious", solo from there to D.C.; unison or 3 parts on D.C.; use 3 part echo if possible.

Bless His Holy Name

(Ps. 103:1-2)

ANDRAÉ CROUCH

A. C.

© Copyright 1973 by Lexicon Music, Inc. ASCAP. All rights reserved. International copyright secured. Used by special permission.

*Arr. © 1986 by Pilot Point Music, Box 419527, Kansas City, MO 64141. All rights reserved.

Bless the Lord, O My Soul

Traditional   (Ps. 103:1)   Traditional

I Will Bless the Lord

(Ps. 145:1-2, 8-9, 17)

F. H.

FRANK HERNANDEZ

*A Song of Thanksgiving Medley

Arr. by Tom Fettke

DOXOLOGY: Choir div.
I WILL BLESS THEE, O LORD: Choir, unison
THOU ART WORTHY: Choir, div.

Doxology

(Ps. 103:20-22)

THOMAS KEN

JIMMY OWENS

Praise God,— from— whom all bless - ings flow; Praise Him,— all crea - tures here— be - low. Praise Him — a - bove, ye heav - en - ly host. Praise Fa - ther, Son, and Ho - ly Ghost. Ghost.

Song ending | Medley ending
New tempo ♩ = 176 (In one)

Suggested introduction

I Will Bless Thee, O Lord

(Ps. 63:4)

Adapted

Anonymous

I will bless Thee, O Lord._____ I will bless Thee, O

Lord._____ With a heart of thanks - giv - ing _____

I will bless Thee, O Lord._____

__ With my hands lift - ed up,_____ and my mouth filled with

praise,_____ With a heart of thanks - giv - ing_____
_____ I will bless Thee, O Lord._____
Lord._____

Song ending

Medley ending

rit.

Thou Art Worthy

(Rev. 4:11)

P. M. M.

PAULINE M. MILLS

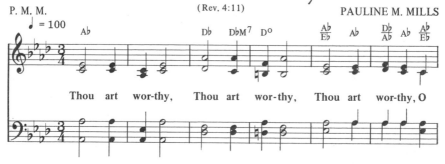

Thou art wor-thy, Thou art wor-thy, Thou art wor-thy, O

71

*Call Him Lord Medley

Arr. by Tom Fettke

I CALL HIM LORD; v.1 and Refrain, div.; v.2, all unison; Refrain, div.
WE'LL CALL HIM JESUS: Div. until double bar ("But when you've . . .") ladies unison from there to
D.C.; D.C., div.
BLESSED BE THE NAME: v.1, men unison; Refrain, all div.; v.4, all div.; Refrain, all unison; use choral
medley tag (div.)

I Call Him Lord

(Song of Sol. 2:1; Is. 9:6; Luke 1:31; John 6:48; 7:37-38; 8:12; 10:9; Phil. 2:9-11; Heb. 13:8; Rev. 22:13,16)

D. R.

DOTTIE RAMBO

1. Mas - ter, Re - deem - er, Sav-ior of the world;
(2. Je -) ho - vah, Mes - si - ah, Might-y God and King;

Won-der - ful Coun-sel - or,___ Bright Morn - ing Star;___
Bread of Life, last -ing words of Love that__ I sing;___

Lil - y of the Val - ley, Pro - vid - er and Friend; He was
Light in dark - ness, Door to heav'n—my home in the sky; The__

yes - ter - day, He'll be to - mor - row, Be - gin - ning and
Foun-tain of Liv - ing Wa - ter that nev - er shall run

End._____
dry._____

REFRAIN

And the an-gel called Him Je -

sus, born of a vir - gin; Mar - y called Him

Je - sus, but I call Him Lord,_____ Je -

2 Song ending
Lord._____

2 Medley ending
Lord._____

Slight accel.

We'll Call Him Jesus

(Is. 9:6; Matt. 1:21, 23)

K. D.

KAREN DEAN

Lyrics:

We'll call Him Je - sus, the name the an - gels whis - pered. We'll call Him Je - sus, come from heav'n to be our Friend. We'll call Him Je - sus, ___ the sweet -est name in all the world. We'll call Him Je - sus, He'll save us from our

2nd time to Coda

Blessed Be the Name

(Ps. 113:2; Is. 9:6; Phil. 2:9-11; Heb. 1:3; Rev. 11:15)

W. H. CLARK
Refrain added by Ralph E. Hudson

RALPH. E. HUDSON
Arr. by William J. Kirkpatrick

CODA

We'll call Him Je - sus; He'll save us from our sin.

Song ending
sin.

Medley ending
sin.

♩ = 112

1. All praise to Him who reigns a - bove In maj - es - ty su - preme,
2. His name a - bove all names shall stand, Ex - alt - ed more and more,
3. Re - deem-er, Sav - ior, friend of man Once ru - ined by the fall,
4. His name shall be the Coun - sel - or, The might-y Prince of Peace,

Who gave His Son for man to die, That He might man re -
At God the Fa - ther's own right hand, Where an - gel - hosts a -
Thou hast de - vised sal - va - tion's plan, For Thou hast died for
Of all earth's king-doms con - quer - or, Whose reign shall nev - er

REFRAIN

deem!
dore.
all.
cease.

Bless-ed be the name, Bless-ed be the name,

Bless-ed be the name of the Lord! Bless-ed be the name,

Song and Medley ending

Bless-ed be the name, Bless-ed be the name of the Lord!

Optional choral medley ending

Lord! Je-sus, Je-sus!

*Great and Wonderful Medley

Arr. by Tom Fettke

GREAT AND WONDERFUL: Unison until "Who shall not", div. from there to D.S.; unison from D.S. to
  end of song.
FOR GOD SO LOVED: v.1 and Refrain, div.; v.3, ladies unison; Refrain, div.
THE TREES OF THE FIELD: Unison

Great and Wonderful

(Rev. 15:3-4)

S. D.

STUART DAUERMANN

Thou._____ Who shall not fear and glo - ri - fy Thy_____ name, O Lord?_____ For Thou a - lone art ho - ly, Thou_____

D.S. al Coda ✝ *CODA* Song ending — *CODA* Medley ending — Same tempo

a - lone._____ men._____ men._____ Smoother

For God So Loved

(John 1:10-12; 3:16-17)

STUART DAUERMANN

S. D.

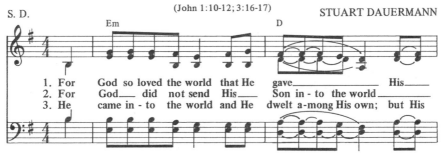

1. For God so loved the world that He gave_____ His_____
2. For God____ did not send His Son in - to the world
3. He came in - to the world and He dwelt a - mong His own; but His

have life___ ev - er - last - ing. For God so loved the world that He
His life___ ev - er - last - ing.

Song ending
Medley ending

gave___ His on - ly be - got - ten Son. Son.

The Trees of the Field

STEFFI GEISER RUBIN
Based on Isaiah 55:12   (Is. 55:12)   STUART DAUERMANN

Play 3 times   You shall go   out   with joy___

___ and be led   forth   with peace;_____   The moun-tains

and the   hills   will   break forth   be - fore you. There'll be

*Jesus Is Lord Medley

Arr. by Tom Fettke

JESUS IS LORD: Use suggested intro.; v.1, choir div.; v.2, ladies, 2 part; Refrain, choir div.
JESUS IS LORD OF ALL: v.1, choir unison; Refrain, choir div. v.2, sop. and ten. duet; Refrain, choir div.
JESUS, LORD TO ME: 1st time, unison choir; 2nd time, div.

Jesus Is Lord

ED SEABOUGH (Rom. 10:9; Phil. 2:9-11) OTIS SKILLINGS

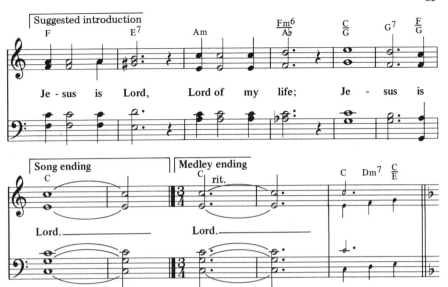

Suggested introduction

Je - sus is Lord, Lord of my life; Je - sus is

Song ending · Medley ending

Lord._____ Lord._____

Jesus Is Lord of All
(Rom. 10:9; Phil. 2:9-11; Rev. 19:16)

GLORIA GAITHER and W. J. G. WILLIAM J. GAITHER

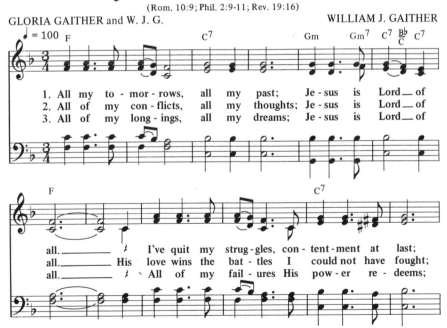

1. All my to - mor - rows, all my past; Je - sus is Lord __ of
2. All of my con - flicts, all my thoughts; Je - sus is Lord __ of
3. All of my long - ings, all my dreams; Je - sus is Lord __ of

all. _____ I've quit my strug - gles, con - tent - ment at last;
all. _____ His love wins the bat - tles I could not have fought;
all. _____ All of my fail - ures His pow - er re - deems;

Jesus, Lord to Me

(Is. 9:6; Rom. 10:9)

G. McS. and G. N.

GARY McSPADDEN and GREG NELSON

*Servant Medley

Arr. by Tom Fettke

LITTLE IS MUCH WHEN GOD IS IN IT: Use suggested intro; v.1, choir unison; Refrain, div.; v.2, solo;
v.3 and Refrain, div.
MAKE ME A SERVANT: Div.
THIS IS MY PRAYER: Choir unison; use choral tag (a cappella preferred)

Little Is Much When God Is in It

(Matt. 9:36-38; 10:42; 25:21; Rom. 12:4-8; 2 Tim. 4:7-8)

K. J. S.

KITTIE J. SUFFIELD

Make Me a Servant

(Mark 10:43-44)

K. W.

KELLY WILLARD

90

This Is My Prayer

(Matt. 16:24; 22:37-38; 2 Cor. 5:14-15)

D. H.

DOUG HOLCK

*Our Great Savior Medley

Arr. by Tom Fettke

HALLOWED BE THE NAME: v.1, div.; v.2, all unison
JESUS, I LOVE YOU: v.1, ladies div.; v.3, all div.
OUR GREAT SAVIOR: v.1, men unison; Refrain, all div.; v.5, all div.; use choral medley tag.

Hallowed Be the Name

(Dan. 2:44; Matt. 6:9; Rev. 5:8-14; 11:15)

L. G.

LILLY GREEN

1st vs. ♩ = 80
2nd vs. ♩ = 84

1. Hal-low-ed   be   the   name____ of   Je-
2. Wor-thy   is   the   Lamb,____ Lord   Je-

sus.____   Ho-ly   is   the   name____ of   Je-
sus.____   Right-teous I   can   stand____ in   Je-

sus.   Oth-er   king-doms rise   and   fall,____ but He
sus.   We were   chained to death,   but   then____ You____

reign-eth   o-ver____ all.____   Hal-low-ed____ be the
raised us   up   a-gain.____   Wor-thy____ is the

Suggested introduction

Jesus, I Love You

(Ps. 116:1; 2 Cor. 5:14-15)

O. S.

OTIS SKILLINGS

1. Je - sus, I love____You, love____You, love____You,
2. Je - sus, I serve____You, serve____You, serve____You,
3. Je - sus, I praise____You, praise____You, praise____You,

Je - sus, I love____You; Je - sus, my Lord.
Je - sus, I serve____You; Je - sus, my Lord.
Je - sus, I praise____You; Je - sus, my Lord.

Lord.

Our Great Savior

(Ps. 107:28-30; Song of Sol. 2:16; Matt. 28:20; John 1:12; 15:13-15; 2 Cor. 1:5; 12:9)

J. WILBUR CHAPMAN

ROWLAND H. PRICHARD

Arr. by Robert Harkness and Tom Fettke

♩ = 112

1. Je - sus! what a Friend for sin - ners! Je - sus!
2. Je - sus! what a Strength in weak - ness! Let me
3. Je - sus! what a Help in sor - row! While the
4. Je - sus! what a Guide and Keep - er! While the
5. Je - sus! I do now re - ceive Him, More than

Lov - er of my soul! Friends may fail me,
hide my - self in Him; Tempt - ed, tried, and
bil - lows o'er me roll, E - ven when my
tem - pest still is high, Storms a - bout me,
all in Him I find. He hath grant - ed

foes as - sail me; He, my Sav - ior, makes me whole.
some - times fail - ing, He, my Strength, my vic - t'ry wins.
heart is break - ing, He, my Com - fort, helps my soul.
night o'er - takes me, He, my Pi - lot, hears my cry.
me for - give - ness; I am His, and He is mine.

REFRAIN

Hal - le - lu - jah! what a Sav - ior!

*We Are So Blessed Medley

Arr. by Tom Fettke

JESUS, WE JUST WANT TO THANK YOU: v.1, choir div.; v.2, duet (sop. and tenor).
WE ARE SO BLESSED: Choir div. until "touch"; unison ladies from "when we're empty" to word
"know"; div. from "we are" to end.
I WILL SERVE THEE: Unison choir until "heartaches"; div. from "heartaches" to end.

Jesus, We Just Want to Thank You

(Ps. 100:4-5; John 14:1-3)

GLORIA GAITHER and W. J. G.

WILLIAM J. GAITHER

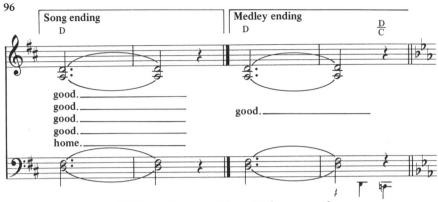

We Are So Blessed

(2 Cor. 5:14-15; Eph. 1:3)

W. J. G. and GLORIA GAITHER

WILLIAM J. GAITHER and GREG NELSON

Arr. by Keith Phillips

We are so blessed by the gifts from Your hand, I just
so blessed, we just can't find a way Or the

can't un-der-stand_____ why You've loved us so much. We are
words that can say,_____ thank You,

Lord, for Your touch. When we're emp-ty_____ You

I Will Serve Thee

(Ps. 116:12-17; John 10:10; 2 Cor. 5:14-15)

GLORIA GAITHER and W. J. G.   WILLIAM J. GAITHER

I will serve Thee___ be-cause I love Thee;___ You have giv-en life to me.___ I was noth-ing___ be-fore You found me; ___ You have giv-en life to me.___ Heart-aches, ___

*Redeemed Medley

Arr. by Tom Fettke

AMAZING GRACE: v.1, div.; v.2, ladies unison, first line—men unison, 2nd line ("How Precious");
v.4, all div.
REDEEMED (Butler): v.1, all unison (or solo); v.2, all unison; Refrain parts and unison as indicated.
REDEEMED (Ganus): v.1, ladies unison; Refrain, all div.; v.2, men unison; Refrain, div.; use medley
ending.

Amazing Grace

(John 1:16-17; 9:25; Rom. 5:20-21; Titus 2:11)

JOHN NEWTON

Early American Melody

1. A - maz - ing grace! how sweet the sound—That saved a
2. 'Twas grace that taught my heart to fear, And grace my
3. The Lord has prom - ised good to me, His word my
4. Through man - y dan - gers, toils, and snares I have al -
5. When we've been there ten thou - sand years, Bright shin - ing

wretch like me! I once was lost but now am found;
fears re - lieved. How pre - cious did that grace ap - pear
hope se - cures. He will my shield and por - tion be
read - y come. 'Tis grace hath brought me safe thus far,
as the sun, We've no less days to sing God's praise

Suggested introduction   **Song ending**   **Medley ending**

Was blind but now I see.
The hour I first be - lieved.
As long as life en - dures.
And grace will lead me home.   home.
Than when we'd first be - gun.

Redeemed

(Gal. 4:4-7; Rev. 5:8-10; 14:3-4)

FANNY J. CROSBY   A. L. BUTLER

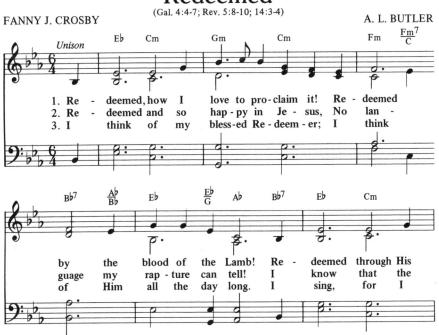

1. Re - deemed, how I love to pro-claim it! Re - deemed
2. Re - deemed and so hap - py in Je - sus, No lan -
3. I think of my bless-ed Re - deem - er; I think

by the blood of the Lamb! Re - deemed through His
guage my rap - ture can tell! I know that the
of Him all the day long. I sing, for I

102

in - fi - nite mer - cy, His child, and for - ev - er, I am.____
light of His pres-ence With me doth con - tin - ual - ly dwell.____
can - not be si - lent; His love is the theme of my song.____

REFRAIN
Sing parts

Re - deemed,____ re - deemed,____ Re - deemed by the__ blood of the

Unison

Lamb;____ Re - deemed thro' His in - fi - nite mer - cy; His

Song ending | Medley ending
accel.

child, and for - ev - er, I am.____ am.____

♩. = 88

Redeemed

JAMES ROWE

(Gal. 4:4-7; Rev. 5:8-10; 14:3-4)

S. A. GANUS
Arr. by Josh McPheeters

1. Sweet is the song _____ I'm sing-ing to - day; I'm re-
(2. Great is my) joy _____ as on-ward I go; I'm re-

deemed! _____ I'm re - deemed! Trou-ble and sor-row _____ have van-ished a-
deemed! _____ I'm re - deemed! All the way home-ward _____ my prais-es shall

way; I have been _____ re - deemed!
flow; I have been _____ re - deemed!

sop. I'm re -

104

*Redeeming Love Medley

Arr. by Tom Fettke

REDEEMING LOVE: Use suggested intro. v.1, solo; Refrain, all div.; v.2, div.; Refrain, all unison—first 2 lines, div. on "My soul shall sing."
LOVE WAS WHEN: v.1, all div.; v.2, ladies unison, all div. on "Love was when Jesus rose."

Redeeming Love

(2 Cor. 8:9; 1 John 4:9-10)

GLORIA GAITHER   WILLIAM J. GAITHER

1. From God's heav-en to a man-ger, from great rich-es to the
2. From a lov-ing heaven-ly Fa-ther to a world that knew Him

poor, Came the ho-ly Son of God, a lit-tle Child.____
not, Came a man of sor-rows, Je-sus Christ the Lord.____

_____ From the az-ure halls of heav-en to a
_____ In my wan-d'ring Je-sus found me, touched my

low-ly man-ger stall, Je-sus came, and here He
life with His great love; And this Babe has grown to

Love Was When

(1 John 4:9-10)

JOHN E. WALVOORD

DON WYRTZEN

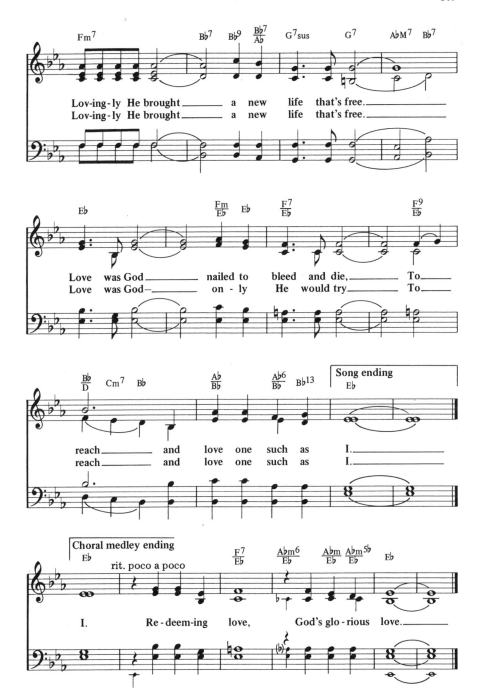

*Christmas Joy Medley

Arr. by Tom Fettke

HOW GREAT OUR JOY: v.1, v.2, div. (use small ensemble for echo).
JOY TO THE WORLD: v.1, ladies 2 part; v.2, all div.
GO TELL IT ON THE MOUNTAIN: Refrain, unison; v.1, div.; Refrain, unison; v.2, solo (or men unison);
Refrain, unison; use choral medley ending (div.).

How Great Our Joy

German Carol

(Luke 2:8-14)

German Carol
Arr. by Hugo Jüngst

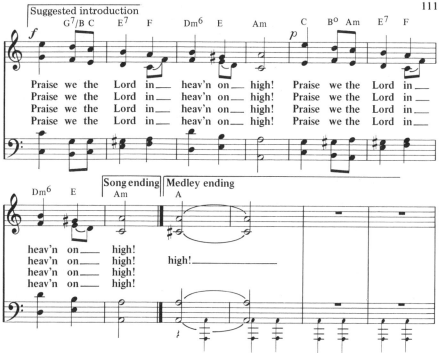

Praise we the Lord in heav'n on high! Praise we the Lord in
Praise we the Lord in heav'n on high! Praise we the Lord in
Praise we the Lord in heav'n on high! Praise we the Lord in
Praise we the Lord in heav'n on high! Praise we the Lord in

Song ending / Medley ending

heav'n on high!
heav'n on high!   high!
heav'n on high!
heav'n on high!

Joy To The World!

(Gen. 3:17-18; Ps. 98; Luke 2:10-11; John 1:17)

ISAAC WATTS   GEORGE F. HANDEL

1. Joy to the world! the Lord is come; Let
2. Joy to the world! the Sav - ior reigns; Let
3. No more let sin and sor - row grow, Nor
4. He rules the world with truth and grace, And

earth re - ceive her King. Let
men their songs em - ploy; While
thorns in - fest the ground. He
makes the na - tions prove The

ev -	'ry heart	pre - pare Him	room,	And
fields and	floods,	rocks, hills, and	plains	Re -
comes to	make	His bless - ings	flow	Far
glo - ries	of	His righ - teous - ness,		And

heav'n and na-ture sing, And heav'n and na-ture sing, And
peat the sound-ing joy, Re - peat the sound-ing joy, Re -
as the curse is found, Far as the curse is found, Far
won-ders of His love, And won-ders of His love, And
And heav'n and na-ture sing,

And heav'n and na-ture

Song ending / Medley ending

New tempo D ♩ = 126

heav'n, and heav'n and na - ture sing.
peat, re - peat the sound - ing joy. joy.
as, far as the curse is found.
won - ders, won - ders of His love.

sing,

Go, Tell It on the Mountain

Traditional Spiritual
Verses: John W. Work, Jr.

(Luke 2:8-20)

Traditional Spiritual
Arr. by Tom Fettke

Unison

Go, tell it on the moun - tain, O-ver the hills and ev-'ry-where.

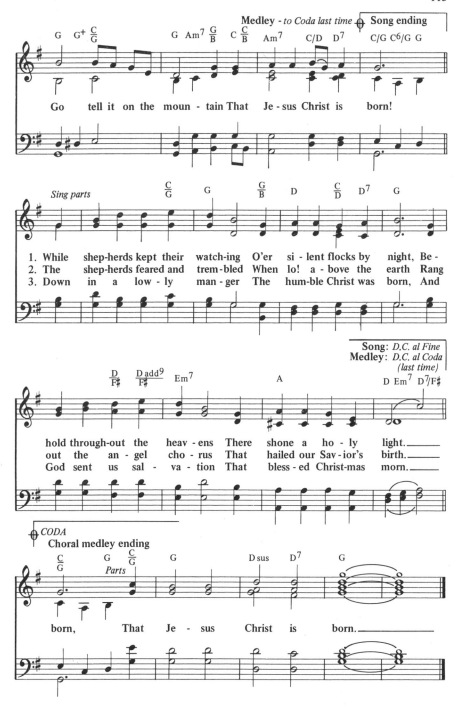

*He Is Here Medley

Arr. by Tom Fettke

OPEN OUR EYES: v.1, choir unison; v.2, all div.
THE LORD IS IN THIS PLACE: Div until double bar; ladies unison "Pray, brothers, pray"; men unison,
   "Pray, sisters, pray"; choir div. from "pray till the mountains" to the end.

Open Our Eyes

(Luke 24:31; John 12:20-21)

B. C.

BOB CULL
Arr. by David Allen

© Copyright 1976 Maranatha! Music. All rights reserved. International copyright secured. Used by permission.

   *Arr. © 1986 by Pilot Point Music, Box 419527, Kansas City, MO 64141. All rights reserved.

The Lord Is in This Place

(Gen. 28:16)

M. L.

MOSIE LISTER

1. Sure - ly, sure - ly the Lord_____ him -
2. Je - sus, Je - sus,_____ Je - sus is

self is in this place._____
here with love and grace._____

A little faster ♩ = 92

Pray, broth-ers, pray;_____ pray, sis-ters, pray;_____

Pray till the moun-tains melt a - way._____ For

Je - sus is near__you and Je - sus will hear__you; For

Song and Medley ending

sure - ly the Lord is in this place._____

*Faithful Father Medley

Arr. by Tom Fettke

MY FATHER WATCHES OVER ME: Use suggested intro.; v.1, unison choir; Refrain, all div; v.2, solo;
Refrain, all div.
GREAT IS THY FAITHFULNESS: v.1 and Refrain, all div.; v.3, ladies unison; Refrain, unison choir;
choral medley tag, all div.

My Father Watches over Me

(Ps. 23:4; 46:1-3; Matt. 6:26; 10:29-31)

W. C. MARTIN

CHARLES H. GABRIEL
Arr. by Tom Fettke

1. I trust in God wher-ev-er I may be,_____ Up-on the land or on the roll-ing sea;_____ For, come what may_____ from day to day,_____ My heav'n-ly Fa-ther watch-es o-ver me.

2. He makes the rose an ob-ject of His care,_____ He guides the ea-gle thro' the path-less air,_____ And sure-ly He_____ re-mem-bers me;_____ My heav'n-ly Fa-ther watch-es o-ver me.

3. The val-ley may be dark, the shad-ows deep;_____ But, oh, the Shep-herd guards His lone-ly sheep;_____ And thro' the gloom_____ He'll lead me home;_____ My heav'n-ly Fa-ther watch-es o-ver me.

118

REFRAIN

Great Is Thy Faithfulness

(Lam. 3:22-23; James 1:17)

THOMAS O. CHISHOLM　　　　　　　　　　　　　　　　WILLIAM M. RUNYAN

1. Great is Thy faith - ful - ness, O God my Fa - ther;
2. Sum - mer and win - ter, and spring-time and har - vest,
3. Par - don for sin and a peace that en - dur - eth,

There is no shad - ow of turn - ing with Thee.
Sun, moon, and stars in their cours - es a - bove,
Thy own dear pres - ence to cheer and to guide;

Thou chang - est not; Thy com - pas - sions, they fail not;
Join with all na - ture in man - i - fold wit - ness
Strength for to - day and bright hope for to - mor - row—

As Thou hast been Thou for - ev - er wilt be.
To Thy great faith - ful - ness, mer - cy, and love.
Bless - ings all mine, with ten thou - sand be - side!

120

*Great and Majestic Medley

Arr. by Tom Fettke

HOW GREAT THOU ART: Use suggested intro.; v.1, all unison; Refrain, div.
I SING THE MIGHTY POWER OF GOD: v.1, 1st 2 lines, ladies unison (opt. div. on "made" and "built");
   v.1, last 2 lines, men unison (opt. div. on "all"); v.2, all div.
HOW MAJESTIC IS YOUR NAME: Unison; div. at "O Lord, we praise" (both times); use opt. choral tag.

How Great Thou Art

(Ps. 96:4-5; 145:3; Rom. 8:32; Rev. 19:4-6)

S. K. H.

STUART K. HINE

1. O Lord, my God, when I in awe-some won-der Con-sid-er
2. When through the woods and for-est glades I wan-der And hear the
3. And when I think that God, His Son not spar-ing, Sent Him to
4. When Christ shall come with shout of ac-cla-ma-tion And take me

all the worlds Thy hands have made,____ I see the stars, I
birds sing sweet-ly in the trees;____ When I look down from
die, I scarce can take it in;____ That on the cross, my
home, what joy shall fill my heart!____ Then I shall bow in

hear the roll-ing thun-der, Thy power through-out the u-ni-verse dis-
loft-y moun-tain gran-deur And hear the brook and feel the gen-tle
bur-den glad-ly bear-ing, He bled and died to take a-way my
hum-ble ad-o-ra-tion And there pro-claim, my God, how great Thou

I Sing the Mighty Power of God

(Gen. 1:1; 1 Chron. 29:11-13; Ps. 19:1; 33:6-8; 95:1-5, 139:7-12; 145:16; Rev. 4:11)

ISAAC WATTS, alt.   from *Gesangbuch der Herzogl,* 1784

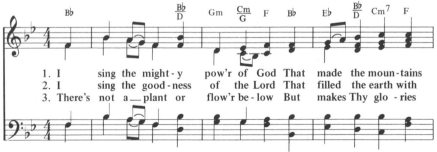

1. I   sing the might-y   pow'r of God That   made the moun-tains
2. I   sing the good-ness   of the Lord That   filled the earth with
3. There's not a—plant or   flow'r be-low   But   makes Thy glo-ries

rise,   That   spread the ___ flow - ing   seas   a -   broad   And
food;   He   formed the ___ crea - tures   with   His ___   word   And
known;   And   clouds a - rise   and   tem - pests ___ blow   By

built ___   the   loft - y   skies.   I ___   sing   the   wis - dom
then ___   pro - nounced them   good.   Lord, ___   how   Thy   won - ders
or -   der   from   Thy   throne;   While ___   all   that   bor - rows

that   or - dained The ___   sun   to   rule the   day;   The moon shines full at
are   dis - played Wher - e'er I turn my   eye: If   I   sur - vey the
life   from Thee   Is ___   ev - er in   Thy care,   And   ev - 'ry - where that

His   com - mand, And   all ___ the   stars   o -   bey.
ground I ___ tread Or   gaze ___ up - on   the   sky!   sky! ___
man   can - be   Thou, God, ___ art   pres - ent   there.

Song ending   **Medley ending**

How Majestic Is Your Name

(Ps. 8:1; Is. 9:6)

M. W. S.

MICHAEL W. SMITH

O Lord,— our Lord,— how ma - jes - tic is Your name— in all——— the— earth. O Lord,—our Lord,— how ma - jes - tic is Your name— in all——— the— earth. O——

Lord, _____ we praise Your name. O__ Lord, _____

_____ we mag - ni - fy_____ Your name: Prince of Peace,_ might-y

God; O__ Lord__ God Al - might - y. O

1
C G C

2 Song and Medley ending
C G C G C

y. _____

Optional choral tag

Lord, how ma-jes - tic (ih) is Your name.

Scripture Reference Index

Topical Index

Alphabetical Index
Song and *Medley* Titles